The Community
Development Challenge

Democracy

The contribution of community development to local governance and democracy

by Melanie Bowles

Published in Great Britain in 2008 by the
Community Development Foundation
Unit 5, Angel Gate
320–326 City Road
London EC1V 2PT
Registered Charity number 306130

British Library Cataloguing in Publication Data
A CIP record for this book is available from the British Library

ISBN 978-1-901974-85-0

Cover design Bearcomm.com, Penzance, Cornwall
Typesetting Third Column, Twickenham
Front cover image: Jeff Sanders
Printed in Great Britain by Crowes of Norwich on paper sourced from
sustainable managed forests

Contents

The Community Development Challenge Working Group members

Maureen Alderson, *Local Government Information Unit*
Gabriel Chanan, *Community Development Foundation*
Jan Crawley, *Southwest Foundation*
Anne-Marie Curry, *London Borough of Southwark*
Jane Dobie, *Community Development Foundation*
Kevin Dykes, *London Borough of Southwark*
Jenny Fisher, *Community Development Foundation*
Alison Gilchrist, *Community Development Foundation*
Amanda Greenwood, *Community Development Exchange*
Jayne Humm, *Community Development Foundation*
Dean T. Huggins, *Ubuntu* and *Sunderland Black and minority ethnic network*
Helena Kettleborough, *Stockport Borough Council*
Margaret Ledwith, *University of Cumbria*
Beth Longstaff, *Community Development Exchange*
Janice Marks, *Federation for Community Development Learning*
Colin Miller, *Independent Consultant*
Phillip Morgan, *TPAS*
John Stevens, *CDSE: Community Development South East*
Mandy Wilson, *COGS*
Alice Wilcock, *Community Development Foundation*

The Community Development Challenge Series Introduction

Empowerment: the essential contribution of community development

Empowerment, under one name or another, has been an objective of social policy for several decades, but it has never had such a specific and high profile commitment in policy agendas as now. It is being promoted as a key concept in the way forward to a more healthy, inclusive and fully-functioning society, and is being included in policy developments applied to the whole population.

How can a major increase in empowerment be achieved? What practical action has to be taken, locality by locality, to bring it about? No single discipline will be enough to achieve the major increase which government is seeking. But it is essential that strategies to accomplish this objective take particular account of the one discipline which has community empowerment as its foremost aim – community development.

This new policy focus on empowerment is an unprecedented opportunity for community development, a discipline with the skills, analysis, methods and experience to engender community empowerment at its very core. Yet for community development to lead the way in this move towards social change, it will itself need major development in order to help address the scale of current policy expectations.

The original *Community Development Challenge* report* posed a dual challenge: to government, local government and other agencies to make better use of community development to achieve empowerment; and to the community development occupation to raise its sights and increase its demonstrable effectiveness.

Community development principles are fundamental to the major issues of our times – social justice and sustainability. But its practice is often limited to local projects and fails to reach its transformative

* CDF, CDX, FCDL and CD2 Working Group (2006) *The Community Development Challenge*, London: Department of Communities and Local Government. Available in hard copy from CDF and downloadable from www.cdf.org.uk

potential in a wider collective context. Where conditions have been favourable, however, it has played a major role in movements for change. For instance, the credit union movement as an anti-poverty strategy began as local community development projects which reached out, supporting and training other communities across the UK, linking with the worldwide credit union movement which aims to eliminate loan sharks and develop local economies.

The government's empowerment objectives are focused on a particular measure: an increase in the number of people who feel they can influence decisions in their locality. This has been designated as the core indicator of empowerment, both at local and national level in England, within the local government performance framework for 2008–11 (National Indicator (NI) 4).[†] NI 4 links community development purposes for the first time into the main management framework for local and national government. However, the aims of community development are much more far reaching than can be captured in this single indicator.

Aspects of community development method, particularly strengthening community groups, have spread through their practical usefulness to workers in health, education, safety, youth, faith and support for the role of local councillors. But most community development literature lacks material on strategic issues and questions of infrastructure, issues which are crucial to achieving a more universal impact. How can community development be funded, deployed, managed and evaluated across the whole population of a local authority? How can peripheral approaches be integrated into a highly skilled holistic approach? How can community development approaches most effectively be mainstreamed? This series of reports begin to explore these key questions.

In its first report (see * above), the Community Development Challenge group set out the basic values and principles of community development, with a practical definition, examples of outcomes, discussion of dilemmas, and recommendations on how to raise its visibility and effectiveness to a higher level. In the further work reported here the group looks in more detail at the strategic developments that need to be addressed to achieve this improvement. We hope subsequently to

† See www.communities.gov.uk/publications/localgovernment/nationalindicator

address the matter of how community development is being and should be used in relation to social issues such as health, safety, housing and sustainable development.

Community development has traditionally focused on intensive work with small clusters of exceptionally motivated activists. Sometimes the cumulative effect of these has amounted to a huge impact, for example within the anti-racist, anti-poverty, women's and peace movements, and in green, gay and lesbian and disability lobbies – movements that have changed life as we see it. Large numbers of people have also benefited indirectly from the activities of small groups, through acquisition of new amenities, through negotiated improvements in public services, through a raised level of social capital and community cohesion in the local community. But most people and even most public agencies would be unaware of the development work behind these improvements.

In order to construct effective local engagement strategies it is important that local authorities and their partners, including communities themselves, draw deeply from the well of community development principles and experience. We hope that this small series of studies will open the door to aspects of this experience which have hitherto been largely in the shadows.

Gabriel Chanan and Margaret Ledwith
for the Community Development Challenge Working Group

Community Development Foundation (CDF)

CDF is a leading source of intelligence, guidance and delivery on community development in England and across the UK. Our mission is to lead community development analysis and strategy to empower people to influence decisions that affect their lives.

CDF's key aim is to spread ways of building engaged, cohesive and stronger communities and a more effective community sector. We work with government departments, regional and local public agencies and the community and voluntary sectors. We also operate at a European and international level.

We are a non-departmental public body sponsored by Communities and Local Government (CLG) and a charity registered in England and Wales and recognised in Scotland.

Community Development Foundation
Unit 5, Angel Gate
320–326 City Road
London EC1V 2PT

Tel: 020 7833 1772
Fax: 020 7837 6584
Email: admin@cdf.org.uk
Website: www.cdf.org.uk

Executive summary

This report is based on a pilot study carried out over a short timescale (May to September 2007). It involved in-depth semi-structured interviews and phone interviews with practitioners operating in a variety of organisational settings.

The report highlights those aspects of community development practice which make decision-making processes more inclusive, participatory and sustainable. It also demonstrates the value of sharing community development skills – and the knowledge gained through working with communities – with elected representatives, local government officers and other stakeholders in partnerships.

Community development:

- enhances the quality of local governance and democracy
- promotes community empowerment and prepares communities for engaging with structures, partnerships and policies
- prepares partnerships and local government for engaging with communities and increases their receptivity to communities' views
- increases people's confidence and ability to seek solutions and take actions themselves (empowerment)
- heightens people's ability and confidence to hold service providers to account for better services (empowerment)
- raises people's expectations of all aspects of their quality of life (empowerment)
- supports the transformation of public services by working outside of 'silos' and encouraging partners to do the same
- contributes to cultural change within organisations by influencing how colleagues and partners engage with communities

- fosters trust, transparency and accountability
- helps councillors to serve and be accountable to their communities
- improves decision-making processes
- improves the decisions that get made.

Background

Following publication of *The Community Development Challenge*,^ this pilot study was commissioned to demonstrate how community development amplifies community empowerment and participation in relation to local governance and democracy.

What community development workers do

Prepare and support people within communities for engagement

From developing a community empowerment network to conducting a community consultation; from recruiting board members and representatives for partnerships to helping groups to identify and access funding for a community hub, youth shelter or gay centre; community development workers:

- Stimulate community level debates and discussions
- Support community groups with their autonomous agendas and activities (to create 'engageable' communities)
- Clarify issues and support action planning
- Broker relationships between people in communities and people who can help them

^ CDF, CDX, FCDL and the CD2 Working Group (2006) *The Community Development Challenge*, London: Department of Communities and Local Government

- Encourage a wider range of people within communities to become representatives
- Support representatives to be accountable to communities
- Support individual representatives to participate.

Prepare and support public authorities for engaging communities

From supporting officers tasked with engaging communities to helping councillors to host members' area panels or participate in neighbourhood management boards, community development workers:

- Set up and service engagement structures and mechanisms
- Clarify issues and support action planning
- Advise on format for consultations and engagement activities
- Communicate developments (and what has happened to community's contributions) through updates and briefings
- Develop strategies and plans which set out good working practices for engaging communities
- Bring public authorities out to where communities meet (to listen and to speak)
- Brief public authority officers and representatives on developments within communities
- Support individual councillors.

Ensure that engagement is empowering for the people who get involved

From supporting community representatives who are engaged in unequal partnerships, to helping officers to receive and respond to criticisms of services; from groups with conflicting priorities to underserved groups who want to influence decisions; community development workers:

- Focus on the values of equity, accessibility, participation and sustainability
- Address power imbalances and support communities to influence decisions
- Work positively with division and dissent
- Challenge inequality and promote inclusion and participation.

Amplifying community development's contribution

The increasing policy focus on community empowerment, and community engagement in local governance and democracy is welcome. The Local Government White Paper (2006) (enacted as the *Local Government and Public Involvement in Health Act* 2007) is a major driver for local authorities and their partners to become more knowledgeable, skilled and effective at interacting with and understanding the communities that they serve. This study demonstrates how community development enhances the quality of local governance and democracy.

Nevertheless some significant constraints on community development need to be recognised and addressed if the White Paper's vision of engaged communities is to be achieved and if community development's potential to enhance local governance and democracy is to be realised.

Actions needed include:

- Give community development the time it takes to build genuine and sustainable empowerment
- Promote better understanding of community development and engagement, and resource internal development within local authorities
- Recognise the opportunity costs of focusing on engagement and resource appropriate development work in communities
- Become increasingly sophisticated in the use of measures for evidencing influence and change.

1 Community development's contribution to democracy and local governance

Community development enhances the quality of local governance and democracy. On the one hand, it promotes community empowerment and prepares communities for engaging with structures, partnerships and policies. On the other hand, it prepares partnerships, local government officers and councillors for engaging with communities and increases their receptivity to communities' views. This report highlights those aspects of community development practice which make decision-making processes more inclusive, participatory and sustainable. It also demonstrates the value of sharing community development skills – and the knowledge gained through working with communities – with elected representatives, local government officers and other stakeholders in partnerships.

In late 2005 Communities and Local Government (CLG) commissioned the report *The Community Development Challenge*,[1] which assesses strengths and weaknesses in the current position of the community development occupation and proposes a range of actions to ensure that it plays a more powerful role in meeting the needs of present-day society. The report emphasises the need to improve the evidence base on community development and make more visible the boosting activities and impacts of community development in creating an environment conducive to an inclusive, democratic and sustainable society.

Following the report's publication, the working group commissioned further research. The pilot study – on local governance and democracy – took place alongside research into community development learning, evaluation and management and strategic working within localities.

1. CDF, CDX, FCDL and CD2 Working Group (2006) *The Community Development Challenge*. London, Department of Communities and Local Government.

2 Our pilot study

The study set out to demonstrate how community development amplifies community empowerment and participation in relation to local governance and democracy. It was carried out over a short timescale (May to September 2007) and aimed to be illuminating rather than comprehensive in scope.

We selected five practitioners whose practice offered the opportunity to study different aspects of community development in depth, and to distil learning. We identified the examples and insights they had to share by asking them to complete a short questionnaire in which they ranked different aspects of practice in terms of their importance in their own work. We decided to use a limited number of participants so that we could explore a cross-section of practice processes, impacts, success factors and challenges. We are indebted to the practitioners for sharing and reflecting on their work in such detail.

The practitioners work in a variety of organisational settings. One practitioner is the first community development (CD) worker to be employed by his organisation; others work in established small teams or within a team of ten CD officers. The resources available for, and expectations of, community development across the settings therefore also vary considerably. Two practitioners work for community empowerment networks (CENs) and are employed by voluntary sector organisations. One works for the housing department of a local authority; two work in local authority CD teams.

Throughout the rest of the report we refer to them either as community empowerment network practitioner (two practitioners) or local authority practitioner (three practitioners).

We conducted in-depth, semi-structured, reflective interviews with the practitioners. Their reflections were supplemented by conducting phone interviews with other involved people for each case study. Seven phone interviews were carried out: with two community activists, a director of a local strategic partnership (LSP), a director of a council for voluntary service (CVS), a local authority corporate director, a local authority service manager, and the community development manager of a lesbian, gay, bisexual and transgender (LGBT) organisation. These phone interviews proved invaluable for drawing out views about community development practice and its impact from a range of points in the local democracy landscape. The interviewees' quotes and examples are included in this report.

3 What do community development workers do?

Community development workers carry out six progressive practice components

The Community Development Challenge (see footnote 1, p. 1 above) identifies six components of community development:

1. Help people see that they have common concerns about local or other public issues and they could benefit from working on them together under their own control.

2. Help people to work together on those issues, often by forming or developing an independent community group, supporting them to plan and take actions, and encouraging evaluation and reflection as a way of improving effectiveness.

3. Support and develop independent groups across the community sector, non-directively but within an ethical framework, and increase networking between groups.

4. Promote values of equity, inclusiveness, participation and cooperation throughout this work.

5. Empower people and their organisations to influence and transform public policies and services and all factors affecting the conditions of their lives.

6. Advise and inform public authorities on community perspectives and assist them to strengthen communities and work in genuine partnership with them.

This study deliberately set out to identify and analyse practice relating to local governance and democracy. It is therefore not surprising that the five case study practitioners were largely focused on community engagement. Many of their practice examples related to components 5 and 6 in the above list: enabling people in communities to contribute to and influence public policies and services, and advising and informing public authorities on how to reach out to, and work with, communities. However, the full picture of their practice is much richer and more diverse than this suggests.

To compare practice within the case studies with the six progressive components above, the practitioners were asked to identify only those components they personally carried out as a major part of their practice, and then to rank these according to their importance in their practice.

Community development workers tailor their practice to suit local context

Each practitioner ranked a different component as the most important in their practice. On first impressions this might suggest confusion about purpose and role. However, the in-depth interviews revealed this to be essential flexibility that enables community development to contribute to local governance and democracy across wide-ranging contexts. Some practitioners were able to focus on particular components because colleagues from their own agency carried out the others. Others deliberately focused on different components to their peers within partner agencies in order to ensure that all types of appropriate community development support were available to groups, partnerships and agencies.

Community development values determine how practitioners operate, and distinguish community development from other services delivered in communities

Furthermore, the only component that all five practitioners highlighted as major in their practice was number 4: promoting values of equity, inclusiveness, participation and cooperation. This shows that 'what' practitioners do will vary according to the infinitely varied contexts in which they are operating. However, the principles that community development practitioners apply are the same across all contexts. This determines 'how' they practise, in the sense that they work to establish trusting relationships based on openness, honesty and respect. A major aspect of their work must always be about challenging inequality, countering discrimination, widening participation and promoting cooperation. This is revisited and expanded on page 9.

Community development supports groups' own agendas and autonomous activities in order to create 'engageable' communities

The range of practice taking place under components 1–3 highlights the importance of providing development support for communities to work autonomously on their own issues, in order to create 'engageable' communities for policy and service decisions. This was backed up by the in-depth interviews in which practitioners reflected on an incredible breadth of work with communities. Stimulating community level debates and discussions, for example, saw practitioners developing networks, supporting consultations, analysing results, training activists in visioning techniques, running and facilitating events, informing people about LAAs and evaluating how informed people felt. Supporting community groups with their autonomous activities saw practitioners establishing clarity on issues, providing project planning and project management support, helping the group to function effectively, writing and delivering customised training and liaising with agencies, organisations and individuals that could help.

While authorities can tend to see groups such as tenants' and residents' associations as part of 'their' engagement structures and mechanisms, these are autonomous independent organisations, where the bulk of the work goes on out of the gaze of the engaging body.

> 'Housing management, in the past, has seen tenants' and residents' associations as their property. They don't see them as independent groups. It's like when they're talking to them about housing management they exist. When they stop talking to them about housing management they don't exist any more.'
>
> *Local authority practitioner*

The bulk of community groups' activities are, like an iceberg, below the surface of the water as far as statutory authorities and partnerships are concerned. So too is the seemingly invisible development work that supports and sustains them. Furthermore, the bulk of this development work is not done by the type of practitioner included in our pilot study. Capacity building for community groups is often carried out by organisational development workers from infrastructure organisations such as CVS, or very locally-based community development workers. These workers are often quite distant from strategic engagement activities, but their work is crucial to sustaining a vibrant voluntary and community sector that is 'engageable'. This makes it even less visible to policy and decision makers, who might dangerously assume that empowerment and engagement automatically and inevitably happen when opportunities for engagement are provided.

Community development workers operate within and across different arenas, and support a range of stakeholders

This section describes the actions community development workers undertake and interactions they support in order to facilitate engagement and empower communities. It highlights the range of stakeholders with which practitioners work and outlines some of the methods they use. The different aspects of workers' practice have been grouped together under three headings: within communities, within authorities and between and across settings.

Within communities

These aspects of community development practice **prepare and support people within communities** for engagement in local governance and democracy.

Community development workers support activists who want to start a group, activists who want help to achieve their group's goals, activists who want to network with other groups, activists who want to influence decisions about their community, representatives chosen to interact with authorities on behalf of their community, and people who live in communities who want to know what has happened about their concerns and ideas.

Within authorities

These aspects **prepare and support public authorities** for engaging local people in local governance and democracy.

Community development workers support officers whose role includes engaging communities or developing a strategy, policy or programme who would benefit from engaging with communities, senior officers who interact with community representatives at partnership tables, councillors who host members' area panels and allocate members' initiative funding, backbench councillors who want support to achieve their community's or group's goals, frontbench councillors who hold a committee or cabinet brief in a service area, and councillors who interact with community representatives at partnership tables.

Between and across settings

These aspects provide the **active and value-driven mediation** between the people who are interacting. Providing opportunities for involvement and engagement does not guarantee that involvement and engagement will happen, or that it will be equitable, accessible, participative or sustainable. These aspects of practice seek to ensure that engagement is as empowering as possible for the people who do get involved.

Community development workers support community activists and representatives to participate as equals in partnerships and to articulate concerns and criticisms of services. They also work with officers who have to receive and respond to criticisms of services, groups with conflicting priorities, groups with historical grievances, groups that feel threatened by difference or change, elected members who feel threatened by representatives on partnerships and boards, underserved groups that want to influence decisions, officers who need to engage underserved groups and officers who have to devise a strategy, plan or programme who haven't considered the needs of underserved groups.

Dimensions of community workers' practice

Communities

Prepare and support people within communities for engagement.

- Community debates
- Community projects
- Brokering relationships
- Awareness raising
- Representatives' accountability
- Representatives' participation

Between

Ensure that engagement is empowering for the people who get involved.

- Shifting power and enhancing influence
- Mediating division and dissent
- Promoting equality and inclusion

Authorities

Prepare and support public authorities for engaging communities.

- Engagement structures
- Advice on engagement
- Communication
- Strategies and plans
- Brokering links
- Support to councillors

Community development workers prepare and support people within communities for engagement

The community development workers participating in the study are active in a range of community engagement settings: from developing a CEN to conducting a community consultation; from recruiting board members and representatives for partnerships to helping groups identify and access funding for their autonomous activities.

The grassroots community projects and autonomous activities they support include a community hub, parents' and toddlers' group, youth shelter, gay centre, church hall, community hall, neighbourhood library, street scheme, cross-borough youth provision and parents' group.

The types of roles they fulfil in these settings include:

- Stimulating community level debates and discussions (for example, developing networks; facilitating consultations, conferences, participatory workshops and events; training in visioning and techniques; supporting issue-based groups; informing people about processes and structures for engagement).

- Supporting community groups with their autonomous activities (for example, clarifying issues; project planning and management; group dynamics and roles; writing and delivering training; providing a range of opportunities for involvement; liaising with partners; identifying political allies).

- Brokering relationships between people in communities and those who can help them.

- Encouraging a wider range of people within communities to become representatives.

- Supporting representatives to be accountable to communities (for example, rejuvenating structures; assessing who is not represented; identifying what structures and representation are needed; helping groups communicate with the wider community).

- Assisting individual representatives to participate (for example, assessing individuals' needs; training and development; translating between strategic and grassroots language).

Community development workers prepare and support public authorities for engaging with communities

The practitioners we interviewed work to support a range of engagement mechanisms and structures for local governance and democracy, including LSPs, neighbourhood management boards, community partnerships, neighbourhood networks, community empowerment networks, tenants' and residents' associations, compact agreement monitoring groups, members' area panels, area action partnerships, local involvement networks (LINks) and community safety partnerships.

The types of roles they fulfil in these settings include:

- Setting up and servicing engagement structures and mechanisms (for example, organising events; supporting structures and forums to run meetings and events; developing governance structures, protocols and procedures and ensuring these fit the local context; preparing partners for joint planning and delivery; preparing reports and recommendations; negotiating and linking up with other structures).

- Advising on formats for consultations and engagement activities (for example, designing a visioning process and training people to carry it out; providing facilitator training; persuading services to start with a blank sheet of paper; analysing purpose of engagement; choosing participatory methods that will achieve purpose; advising on small local engagement activities instead of one central event; advising local authority services on how to engage with communities).

- Communicating developments (and what has happened to the community's contributions) through updates and briefings.

- Developing strategies and plans which set out good working practices for engaging communities (for example, community development strategy; community engagement strategy; convening a community engagement working group across all key statutory and voluntary agencies).

- Bringing public authorities out to where communities meet and discuss (to listen and to speak).

- Briefing public authority officers and representatives on developments within communities.

- Supporting individual councillors (for example, providing a sounding board; promoting and administering funding; providing items, information and reports for members' area panel meetings; advising on how to communicate opportunities and limitations of programmes; helping councillors progress community projects).

Community development ensures that engagement is empowering for the people who get involved

While other professionals could set up and service engagement structures, community development values and principles motivate community development workers to address imbalances of power, influence, inequality and conflict.

The types of roles community development workers fulfil in these settings include:

- Shifting power and enhancing influence (for example, developing the 'axis of influence'[2] tool with networks and groups, using participatory methods in events and meetings to even out power relationships).

2. This was commissioned from Changes to measure groups' readiness to influence. More details on www.dosti.org.uk . See also page 15 below.

- Mediating division and dissent (for example, between community groups, elected members and community representatives, service providers and community representatives; by acknowledging differences and grievances; anticipating and exploring the causes of tensions; helping people to work out how they'll respond to conflict; helping to agree common goals; mediating conflicting priorities; fostering relationships based on trust).

- Promoting equality, inclusion and participation (for example, using participatory methods; asking who is not in the room and how can we include them; focused work on the needs and experiences of underserved groups; infrastructure support for underserved groups; equalities training; equality and diversity monitoring).

Community development workers clarify issues and support action planning

'Clarifying issues' and 'action planning' were key roles and skills in the community development practice of the five practitioners we interviewed.

One practitioner described his approach as being like 'peeling an onion'. Wherever an idea, problem or issue originates, the practitioner's approach is to work with the group, partnership or community to tear away the layers to find out the core issues and then plan some very practical actions. This action plan forms the group's agenda every time they meet until it is achieved, and progress is marked to show forward movement.

Community development workers apply the same analytical skills to their work with partnerships and statutory authorities as they do with community groups and networks.

A practitioner helped a local partnership to analyse the purpose of a planned conference and associated workshops and to choose methods that would achieve that purpose. She demonstrated the benefits of moving away from presentations, to pairs and small group activities feeding back on key points. She helped the partnership to work out what outcomes needed to be recorded (for policy formulation purposes) and what information could be shared in advance, instead of recording every interaction on the day.

Across all areas of work, digging deeper, political analysis and not taking things at face value are essential elements of community development workers' practice (see pages 23 and 24). They can be objective in clarifying issues and planning actions. They are not the community, the service, or the partnership. However, this is not the same as taking a neutral standpoint, as community development values are fundamental to the way people practise and explicitly set out to promote social justice through challenging discrimination and oppression, addressing power imbalances and inequality.[3]

Community development workers address power imbalances and support communities to influence decisions

Whether preparing individual representatives for meetings or setting up and servicing engagement structures, community development workers focus explicitly on redressing imbalances of power and influence. They use political analysis to assess how formal and informal power and representative and participatory democracy interact. They attune community groups to thinking about who holds power and what they are hoping to achieve through influence.

3. Federation for Community Development Learning and PAULO (2003) *National Occupational Standards for Community Development Work*: Sheffield, FCDL.

A CEN practitioner commissioned the development of an 'axis of influence' evaluation tool to use in supporting local networks and groups. This now helps them define their current stage of influence, what they are, and are not, ready for, and what they are trying to influence. It introduces indicators that groups can use continually to review and evaluate their progress and the difference they're making.

Community development practitioners adopt working methods that rebalance different levels and kinds of power.

To even out power relationships in the meetings she convenes, one practitioner replaced the traditional meeting format with participatory methods. Dominant voices are diluted and quieter voices encouraged. The group is often split into smaller groups for different 'speeds of involvement'.

The practitioners' working methods lead directly to empowerment outcomes as all participants are encouraged to bring their own knowledge and experience to the fore, and community activists and representatives are enabled to see themselves as part of the solution (see further examples on pages 13 and 14).

Community development workers work positively with division and dissent

Wherever you are in the local governance and democracy landscape there is potential for conflict, and the support of a community development worker is invaluable for acknowledging and addressing division and dissent. Acknowledging grievances between community groups and helping them to see and agree common goals is essential in any development role. Similarly, fostering relationships based on trust between communities and authorities depends on a community development worker's ability to take people's experiences seriously, acknowledge where things have gone wrong and seek improvements.

A practitioner prepared service providers for engaging with communities by delivering facilitator training. The service providers were advised to begin their engagement activity by asking what participants disliked. This would give people from communities the space to make an emotional response before moving on to talk about their 'likes' and ideas for the future. Service providers attending the facilitator training were also asked to anticipate potential areas of tension and conflict. They were supported to consider and practise how they would respond if their service was criticised. This preparation enabled them to accept criticism without being put on the spot or shutting down valuable dialogue and learning.

Within one neighbourhood, extensive community consultation has identified 'youth facilities' as the number one development priority, but an active and organised pressure group is preventing facilities being sited near their houses. The community development worker is mediating the conflicting priorities between different groups, different generations and residents of different streets within the neighbourhood and is working with the councillors who can approve or veto decisions. He has made contact with an independent organisation from outside the geographical area that has facilitated similar work in other neighbourhoods.

Community development workers are well placed to mediate or work positively with conflict, because of their social justice value base. Theirs is an active, not a neutral mediation, but is all the more important for the emphasis that community development places on overcoming disadvantage and discrimination.

Because of their voting powers and responsibility, councillors can often be caught up in conflict situations. Views will sometimes crystallise along party political lines, but at other times the threat or conflict comes from the mechanisms and structures of local governance and participatory democracy. For example, LSP decisions on highways might subsequently be overturned by a council committee or cabinet (or vice versa). Interviewees cited neighbourhood management mechanisms as a source of further tension and conflict, treading on the toes of both councillors and community groups, because of a failure to establish what that mechanism adds – in practice – to the local governance and democracy landscape of a particular locality. Community development workers, with their knowledge of local communities and analytical skills can help neighbourhood management teams to understand how they can fit into and enrich local community activity, and to analyse and articulate their USP.

Community development workers challenge inequality and promote inclusion and participation

Community development workers promote inclusion and participation through always asking themselves 'who else isn't in this room, why not, and how can we include them?'. They then respond in a variety of imaginative ways in order to take positive action to challenge inequality and discrimination.

In order to maximise the 'reach' of a community strategy consultation, a CEN practitioner provided visioning training for activists who then delivered visioning workshops in their own groups and networks. This simple approach reached more than 50 community groups, including a church congregation and a group of Asian women.

Community development workers are able to pick up on issues causing fear or concern within communities, and address them through equalities training or informal approaches. One of the practitioners interviewed had seen the burning issues within the groups she supports change from a focus on HIV/AIDS, to mental health/care in the community, to asylum and immigration. In each case she was able to alleviate fears, challenge discrimination, raise awareness and provide support.

A community development worker wanted to ensure that the access issues and experiences of people with learning and physical disabilities were taken into account in a regeneration consultation. In advance of the consultation he commissioned a DVD that gathered and presented their views in a comprehensive and compelling format. The DVD was circulated to other targeted local stakeholders in order to raise their awareness about the significance of these access issues in relation to their own service area.

Community development workers promote positive action by providing infrastructure support for underserved groups, so that services' increasing realisation that they need to engage them is mirrored by a corresponding increase in the underserved groups' capacity to be engaged. One example is of community development support to plan, resource, establish and support LGBT infrastructure development:

> '[The practitioner's] work in getting the service providers all round the same table has helped them see the benefits of a holistic approach to consultation and involvement. There is the potential for this hub to work across all equality, diversity, inclusion, consultation, health, mental health and sexual health issues. One small piece of work on gender equality has already had an impact across all levels of authority. It will work better for [our organisation] than individual calls one by one. The danger that way is of a schism through over-consultation.'
>
> *Community development manager of an LGBT group*

What does community development add to local governance and democracy?

Community development increases people's confidence and ability to seek solutions and take actions themselves (empowerment)

> 'In terms of individual empowerment, focusing on dialogue assists people to bring their own knowledge and experience to the fore, so they're not passive listeners to a supposed expert. This is empowering in itself as they become valued contributors.'
>
> *CEN practitioner*

This can, in turn, encourage people to become engaged on an ongoing basis, either on a service-initiated engagement process or within a partnership, or on an autonomous community project. Providing this range or pyramid of involvement opportunities is crucial. From simply putting your views forward at an event, to representing a network of networks on a strategic partnership, all levels of engagement opportunity need to be open. Community development supports people to develop skills and confidence at their chosen level of involvement, and supports them to progress through levels if they choose.

> 'There was a time when I was just filling my time. I hated simple things like talking on the phone, and doing paperwork. Other people in the group were the same as myself. Now it's about seeing the fruition of our work.'
>
> *Community activist*

> 'If you were coming in cold to the partnership you wouldn't be able to tell who were the professionals and who were the community

representatives, if it wasn't for the nameplates. Community sector partners have got the confidence to engage. They see themselves as part of the solution, not just asking things of service providers.'

LSP director

As well as the **individual empowerment** of the activists involved, community development support leads to the **realisation of practical projects**, which make a difference to people's lives.

A community development worker provided a sounding board for ideas, worked alongside the group to undertake a huge community consultation, walked the group through group roles, fundraising and managing accounts, provided project planning support for a local development, and negotiated with other departments and services within the council on the group's behalf. There is now a larger, more active group of residents, and a new community facility where there used to be a boarded-up shop-front. 'If [the community development worker] hadn't turned up that wouldn't have happened.'

Community activist

'So the community hub [a building] has become an answer in itself. It's where stuff happens, but it's also where you talk about the other stuff that could happen.'

Local authority practitioner

Other tangible projects realised with community development support include after-school provision, facilities for parents and toddlers, a re-furbished church hall used by community groups, a community hall and cross-borough youth provision. These are not only important services in the community; they also provide communal spaces for interaction and safe informal opportunities for dialogue, debate and mutual support.

Furthermore, practitioners and activists alike are proud of the **wider empowerment impacts** of their activities.

In 2006 a local authority commissioned consultants to undertake a housing and neighbourhood survey with residents. One 'empowerment' question asked residents the extent to which they believed they had influence on decisions affecting their neighbourhood. Across the whole survey area 28% of residents agreed they could influence decisions affecting their neighbourhood, while 40% disagreed. In the only neighbourhood where community development was being delivered continually and intensively, 51% of residents agreed they could influence decisions affecting their neighbourhood while only 25% disagreed.

Community development heightens people's ability and confidence to hold service providers to account for better services (empowerment)

The policy focus on neighbourhood renewal introduced requirements for LSPs and neighbourhood management (from 2001, in the 88 most deprived areas of England). It beckoned in a new era of local area agreements and community calls for action (introduced in the Local Government White Paper, 2006[4]). The essence of neighbourhood renewal is about narrowing the gap between service delivery in the most deprived areas of England and the rest of the country.[5] The practitioners in our pilot study reflected on the importance of community development support both in raising expectations of services and in developing a collective voice and infrastructure to articulate these expectations to authorities.

4. Communities and Local Government (2006) *Strong and Prosperous Communities: The Local Government White Paper*. London, CLG.
5. Cabinet Office (2001) *A New Commitment to Neighbourhood Renewal: National Strategy Action Plan*. London, Cabinet Office.

In a local authority with mature engagement and involvement structures and a tradition of community development support for community involvement, residents simply expect to be involved in decisions that will affect them, and participation levels are high. Community development workers help people within communities to marshal the evidence and sift the competing priorities. Community representatives routinely make considerable input to governance and decision making on practical issues such as priorities and timescales for a programme of works, and influence policymaking through involvement and campaigning. Collectively they have considerably raised expectations of the council's performance and driven up service standards.

One LSP harnessed the considerable skills and experience of equalities and black and minority ethnic network members of the local CEN. Representatives of the networks worked with the LSP board to frame (and not simply critique) work on narrowing the gap in service delivery between mainstream and marginalised communities. They focused on areas where inequality persists nationally, analysed local features and framed locally-appropriate responses.

For people within communities to be and feel empowered, belonging to a group or collective groundswell is absolutely essential:

> 'Without the structures behind you, you're just a resident who's unhappy.'
>
> *Local authority practitioner*

> 'If an individual makes a phone call [about planned developments in his or her neighbourhood] they don't get anywhere, whereas providing a network gives a collective voice and someone from the service will come out to a network meeting that covers that area.'
>
> *CEN practitioner*

> 'The structure of the community empowerment network in our area as a network of networks is a major strength, and a good example that would be well-followed by others. Four seats on the LSP board are available to [the CEN] and we don't make the distinction between the voluntary and community sector. Any member of [the CEN] could sit there, irrespective of "status".'
>
> *LSP director*

Supporting networks and representatives to hold councils to account with constructive criticism drives up service standards, provides services with greater reach and access to communities' views, creates opportunities for participation in community level debates and discussions and reaches communities at places where they meet anyway. Nevertheless, the community development workers providing this support can risk being scapegoated or branded troublemakers by partnerships, councillors or officials who do not fully understand or believe in these positive impacts.

> 'Some of the councillors in our authority misunderstand community development and think it's all about left-wing agitation; as if we've got magic batteries we put into residents' backs to get them to stir up trouble, where there was none before.'
>
> *Local authority practitioner*

While sometimes branded as agitators or troublemakers, community development workers provide an essential and invaluable role in bringing together community groups and service deliverers with different starting out points. Ignoring residents doesn't make them go away. Shutting stakeholders out of debates or silencing them stores up resentment and entrenches positions further. Bringing people together and facilitating dialogue develops mutual respect and trust.

'We did get someone from planning to go to the network meeting that covers [that area] to answer questions about the planning application for the regeneration development. The guy from planning turned round and said, "I was expecting to get crucified, but that went really well." And the people that had attended the meeting said, "That went alright, didn't it? It's answered our questions and that's helped".'

CEN practitioner

Community development raises people's expectations of all aspects of their quality of life (empowerment)

Increased confidence to take action and heightened ability to hold service providers to account combine to produce another, third, dimension of empowerment. As a result of sustained community development support to groups, networks and participatory democracy movements, people learn to give and expect more in all aspects of their community life.

Training tenants' and residents' associations on supporting vulnerable people has increased residents' willingness to extend neighbourliness and involvement in their organisations to vulnerable people and people with mental illness, and to seek external service provision or support if a crisis arises.

Their expectations go beyond raised expectations of their council's performance in a particular service area, to expectations of a more equitable and diverse community.

'For every area of their lives there's a powerful person or agency somewhere. Somewhere to go for action.'

Local authority practitioner

With this raised awareness of decision-making processes and heightened skills at analysing their particular perspective and representing their views, the empowerment effect extends to other, broader areas of society.

Community development supports the transformation of public services by working outside of 'silos' and encouraging partners to do the same

Community development acts as a golden thread, running across all service areas and issues addressed by community strategies and LAAs. While public service officers will naturally look at the part of the strategy or agreement relevant to their own work, community development workers look at the impact of these services on communities, neighbourhoods and underserved groups. This broadens partnership discussions, debates and decision making to their intended, holistic, 'quality of life' considerations.

Community development workers observe that, currently, this broadening happens while partners are together 'round the table', but when they return to their organisations partners do what they were going to do anyway, and the 'silo mentality' creeps back in.

To counteract this slipping back to established patterns and entrenched positions, one practitioner explicitly prepares partners for the purpose of the partnership meeting or collaborative event. She asks them to think about the issue in advance, for example, and to come prepared with what they will be able to contribute to addressing it. She asks them ***not*** *to talk about delivery they are doing anyway, but to identify the extra joint work and joint delivery that working in partnership enables.*

Community development teams often influence the ideas and wording of the introductory sections of strategies and agreements, for example outlining the overarching goals of community engagement, community cohesion, pride in one's community or community well-being. They are rarely responsible for individual service delivery targets within the LAA. However, these sections are important in highlighting those matters of importance to communities that individual services don't deliver or have targets around. Furthermore, community development practitioners can show how to engage with geographical *and* underserved communities in order to involve them in accurately identifying local needs, and suggesting ways to reconfigure services to take these into account.

An LGBT steering group, made up of LGBT voluntary groups and public sector partners, is working towards establishing an LGBT infrastructure where limited support is currently available. The local authority has provided ongoing community development support and the worker has understood and addressed the 'territorialism' of partner agencies. All agencies wanted to do, and demonstrate that they were doing, something 'on their patch', whether at district, town, primary care trust or other geographical level. The worker has supported the LGBT groups in asserting the issues of fear, intolerance and discrimination that threaten to undermine very localised solutions and, with the worker's support, the partners have pulled together to develop a 'hub and spoke' approach. The worker has been crucial in keeping key service providers in the process. The value added by a community development worker acting as a golden thread across partnership-working, project planning and project management has been enormous.

Buy-in from partners is crucial and has to be worked at. In the majority of cases the people most challenged by this boundary-spanning community development work will be council colleagues and partners in other services such as highways, estates and corporate services, whose working practices will need to realign substantially to reflect the way that communities want to interact, and central government wants them to engage with communities.

> 'It's the same thing that other people want to achieve. Everyone wants that service to work. Everybody wants to solve the problems in communities. It's just the way in which you do things that makes the difference.'
>
> *Local authority practitioner*

Community development contributes to cultural change within organisations by influencing how colleagues and partners engage with communities

The 2006 Local Government White Paper (see footnote 3 page 14) is the latest in a series of policy developments requiring statutory agencies to engage communities in decisions about public service delivery and community quality of life. Whilst statutory agencies have been continually reorganised in recent years, this increasing focus on local governance and reinvigorating local democracy will require more significant cultural change than redeployment. Where community development workers are employed by local authorities, they are ideally placed to support services to reconfigure and realign, and to advise and support their colleagues on the best methods for engaging with local communities.

Simply employing community development workers doesn't make cultural change happen. Community development teams may need deliberately to restyle their approach to exert maximum influence on internal colleagues.

One local authority community development team reviewed and restyled its approach. It assessed its internal impact as weak and set out to redress the situation by adopting a more balanced split in its work. More time is now spent working internally with council colleagues. There are ten workers in the team, but the council employs thousands of people. The community development team believes it can have a far greater impact on community engagement by advising and supporting a range of colleagues on ways to engage and creating a culture of engagement, than if the team members did most of their work at community level themselves. The team has produced a community development policy and a community engagement strategy that form part of council colleagues' induction process. They present the team's work to other departments, and employ a training officer who runs rolling programmes for councillors and colleagues. Each worker within the team has lead responsibility for a service area (such as corporate services or social services), and policy area (for example, neighbourhood management), as well as a locality and underserved group. Workers meet monthly with the chief officers who are the council's representatives on LSPs to brief them on developments in the communities covered by the partnerships.

A single, newly-created community development worker post was the catalyst in a small local authority for a new look at engaging communities and developing fledgling engagement strategies. Senior managers (directors and assistant directors of services) were accessible, and the chances of impacting on a relatively small staff team were good. Early successes led to the creation of a community development manager post and incorporating outreach workers from elsewhere in the authority into the community development team.

Community development practitioners need to be equally skilled in working at both grassroots and strategic level. This includes their communication skills, but goes beyond that to cover strategic, organisational and political skills.

Community development workers in the voluntary sector can also promote significant cultural change within statutory agencies and partnerships when they demonstrate effective ways of engaging in trusting, honest and open dialogue with communities.

> 'It was really important that [the CEN practitioner] did it. The voluntary sector taught us [the statutory sector] something. We're the heavyweights, we tend to wade in to partnerships, and others shrink down their contribution, because partnerships aren't equal. But here the voluntary sector was leading us and showing their strengths, which inspired a healthy respect. That really added value.'
>
> *Local authority service manager, talking about a CEN practitioner*

> '[The CEN] is always our first thought for any involvement or engagement needs, rather than external consultants. The engagement we can achieve through them is more sustainable and better.'
>
> *LSP director*

Community development fosters trust, transparency and accountability

Fostering relationships of trust is at the heart of what community development workers do, and at the heart of the cultural change they are trying to support within their own and partner organisations. Practitioners' commitment to – and skill in – being honest about limitations is key to building up relationships of trust.

> '[The worker] can take abuse and criticisms and always listens to other opinions.'
>
> *Community activist*

They do this themselves and help others – notably councillors – to be honest about the constraints on development and regeneration programmes.

> 'It turns out that the scheme brings no guarantees of money. I've had to work with the member to communicate that, outside of the [neighbourhood management] board, to make sure that people don't suddenly jump on to it with a different expectation.'
>
> *Local authority practitioner*

Community development practitioners promote transparency by translating from strategic to everyday language, and back again, to ensure that communities, councils and partners all understand each other's needs, processes and priorities.

They support accountability between decision makers, representatives and communities by creating feedback mechanisms and ensuring that they are used. However, the complexity of community development workers' lines of accountability must be recognised, especially where the strategic need and drive to engage communities takes precedence over development work on communities' autonomous and ongoing activities.

> 'It is difficult to manage because what's always a challenge is, "Who is your master?". Community development officers might automatically say, "It's communities, communities, communities." And when I've worked in the voluntary sector – and on regeneration programmes you do have that remit – you are able to be led and steered by community issues alone. As a local authority officer, trying to work across services and policy areas, you are always balancing what the chief officer needs, and what the corporate approach requires, with what the communities need. And I suppose the challenge with that across all these levels is getting the happy medium.'
>
> *Local authority practitioner*

Communication is a key process by which the outcomes of trust, accountability and transparency can be achieved or enhanced. Inauthentic communication, or failure to articulate processes invisible to other stakeholders, erode trust, accountability and transparency.

One LSP branded all its communication about the community strategy as ***The [town] Borough Challenge****. With the advent of LAAs the LSP then dropped the* ***Borough Challenge*** *branding. To the community groups and activists who inputted to the comprehensive community strategy consultation this looked as though their contributions had also been dropped, although the community strategy still underpins the LAA. To try to restore confidence and reassert the link to the community strategy, the CEN independently produced a briefing on the LAA entitled* ***Taking the Challenge Forward****. The LSP director acknowledges that many LAA partners use this briefing in their own organisations when trying to explain the LAA.*

Community development helps councillors to serve and be accountable to their communities

Councillors play a range of roles in relation to the communities they serve. At times they are members of a community trying to get a project off the ground or pressing for improvements in service delivery. At other times they are the council's representatives, breaking good or bad news, managing expectations and protecting the council's reputation. They are hard-pressed volunteers who believe they are carrying out a public service and civic duty. They too can benefit from community development support in all their roles.

A seemingly routine task such as helping councillors to administer the Members Initiative Fund (£2,000 a year) keeps community development workers in constant touch with the members in their designated area including, of course, cabinet members and the leader of the council.

'The politicians are the first people I go to for information in the communities and vice versa. They'll say, "Have you got anything on this?". I always say, "I don't know but I'll find out for you", and generally nine times out of ten I'm able to get to the right person and information from the right enquiry.'

Local authority practitioner

A councillor approached a community development worker for help with a dilapidated church hall that was used by many community groups. The community development worker advised him to set up a hall committee with representatives from the community groups, and helped the groups to function effectively as a single group. The committee involved parishioners in a mini-process for deciding firstly what needed to be done. What would maximise use of the hall by young people and all sections of the community? A feasibility study was done and community development workers from other agencies were brought in to advise on funding. The committee managed to secure funding to refurbish 70% of the hall and held a celebration event to show what it had achieved.

'That was through members saying, "Look, can you come and help out with this?". The conversations are not sophisticated. And then you go and figure out what it is they need. To some degree you can look at the fact that it is an interest of the councillor, rather than a community need, but as with all community development work some analysis, possibly a feasibility study or needs assessment, has to be done to make sure the project's needed and will be worthwhile.'

Local authority practitioner

Community development workers provide this essential linking and checking back with wider communities that enhances accountability and legitimacy in participatory and not just electoral terms. They help councillors to understand their own multiple roles in representing council *and* community and help individuals, groups and partnerships to analyse and negotiate how they converge and differ from each other.

Community development workers advise councillors on ways to create and maintain trusting and transparent relationships with people in their communities.

> 'I think we've got that relationship that says, "well what are you paying us for here? I have to tell you my best advice and not just do whatever you say".'
>
> *Local authority practitioner*

However, they are often brought in to troubleshoot or firefight when something goes wrong, without necessarily being privy to the policy or (party) political decisions in question before they hit the headlines of the local newspaper. Their skills in 'peeling an onion' and political analysis stand them in good stead for looking below the surface of seemingly transparent decisions. Nevertheless this can occasionally lead to the community development worker being caught in political crossfire, for example where support for, or suspicion of, a community 'cause' crystallises along party political lines, rather than reflecting feasibility or community benefit considerations.

Community development improves decision-making processes

Different aspects of community development practice significantly improve decision-making processes. Community development workers use their skills and knowledge to advise partnerships and services on locally appropriate methods of engaging.

A local authority community development team advised the officer responsible for LINks (which are replacing patient and public involvement forums in health) on locally appropriate engagement activities. Each CD worker recommended approaches that would be appropriate for the communities with which they worked. This led to more than 60 engagement activities across the county. This approach reached people where they were active and already networked, instead of requiring them to attend one central meeting or event. It maximised inclusion and participation, and 'delivered' the communities that LINks were seeking to engage.

Community development workers use participatory methods in consultation events, workshops, networking events and meetings to ensure that participants are able to contribute as fully as they wish to the decision-making process. As highlighted earlier, this rebalances power relationships and empowers communities to become part of the solution to problems (co-production).

Community development impacts at all stages in the decision-making cycle. It opens up new ways of setting agendas and defining issues and problems.

A community development worker in a CEN persuaded the LSP and service teams from the local authority to begin their engagement activities with simple open-ended questions instead of a menu of predetermined options.

At the policy formulation and policy implementation stages of the cycle, community development supports broad community engagement through supporting the networks and forums that create 'engage-ability'. Community development improves policy formulation and implementation through advising services (such as housing or planning) and partners on good practice in engagement in order to gather a broader evidence base for decisions. By actively building collective approaches through networking groups, community development helps to generate representation, gets representatives into policy arenas and supports individual representatives to be effective in deliberations and negotiations.

Sometimes the policy being formulated is all about community development, empowerment or engagement, and the community development worker convenes a working group or workshop series with a range of stakeholders in order to establish shared understanding of the key concepts and work towards a shared approach.

> 'One thing that's come to the fore because of the community engagement working group activity is to recognise that even the word "community" is understood in so many different ways by people and even the same person in their working life and in their personal life will think of it differently. So when we talk about "community development" or "community engagement" or "community empowerment", we're not starting with the same basis of who the community is. And if we then look at motivations to engage or empower or develop, they obviously vary and a lot of them are driven by well-embedded cultures and ways of operating in organisations that rub against the new policies that are coming down.'
>
> *CEN practitioner*

Evaluation of policy and implementation decisions should also involve communities, and can therefore benefit from community development support on community engagement.

The example overleaf demonstrates how a community development worker helped community voices in the case study to be heard in the corridors of power and helped service providers to act in response. The worker will help the community to monitor and assess how service providers are doing in the next stage.

Initial questionnaire research identified unmet service needs of LGBT people. To interpret the findings and suggest ideas for meeting needs and aspirations, a focus action group of more than 30 LGBT people was brought together. Their ideas formed the basis of an LGBT centre project, and a steering group consisting mainly of professionals was set up to progress the plans. At the policy formulation and implementation stage the project had community approval but had not been driven by the community. As the plans progressed and the launch of the centre approached, the next stage drew community representation from the focus action group to check how the project was shaping up against the original ideas and aims.

'Squaring the circle will see the focus action group become a monitoring group for the project in the long term.'

Community development manager of an LGBT group

Community development improves the decisions that get made

Community development improves decisions by broadening the evidence base upon which they are made. This takes into account a wider range of perspectives and expertise, and is especially valuable in reaching and learning from underserved communities. With or without community development, communities have considerable influence over the decisions that get made if they choose to exercise it collectively.

'[The local authority] were looking to obtain several million in regeneration for housing. They did this report and proposal and said they'd spoken to communities about it, and they had only really spoken to community representatives on small elements within it. But they claimed they'd got the remit of communities. It all came out because of rumour and the report being published and some of the councillors found out about it, and it suddenly became

> a very hot potato. All the community were saying, "They're going to pull our houses down". So you can imagine 250 people turn up at the next meeting with a noose for the leader of the council. And that was community action in reality and it just shows the power of community action, though it isn't used that often. And that's a very recent incident, that's this year's topic. And what they had to do was get new consultants in and redo the whole bid based on community need.'
>
> *Local authority practitioner*

Community development channels communities' energy into pursuing the best possible outcomes for them. It encourages buy-in from all stakeholders, by helping everyone in the process to explore and identify what the best possible outcome entails.

> 'We're always saying to services "It's fine to take that approach to consultation, but if in the long term you included people from within those communities, if in the long term you looked at the bigger picture, then you'd get a better future, a better outcome." I think that's a big thing with this [town centre] development that I'm working on at the moment. It's £25 million in private investment. But we as a council and as a local community need to ask how it fits in with the tradition of the area. What kind of quality of build are we going to have? How is it accessible for people? These questions are all about sustainability, rather than just taking it because it's £25 million. So we can often be in the middle of two trains of thought, "we need it" versus "we need the best out of it".'
>
> *Local authority practitioner*

Community development can help communities to place a different emphasis on, or add an extra dimension to, something that would exist anyway, such as a housing investment programme or a local area agreement. It can help communities to drive up standards through reports and recommendations which reflect their views on service issues such as systems for managing council property, charging leaseholders or allocating properties. It helps communities to articulate, and service providers to recognise, that the place where all their different policies, strategies and targets really join up is at the community level.

> 'For example, we're doing some work on people's well-being. Well-being is one of the words that comes on "our" page of the community strategy. It reflects the feeling that came from people's post-its, and we talked about how, for every decision that partnerships make, we should be asking the question, "What impact does this have on community well-being, on people's well-being?" Because I don't think they think like that. It's giving us another opportunity to bring the agenda back to people, not services.'
>
> *Community empowerment network practitioner*

Community development can also help communities to engage in a way which significantly changes decisions by leading to a new way of looking at the same goal (for example, town centre regeneration).

The corporate services department of a local authority approached a community development worker (CDW) to see how he could help with a regeneration project the department were developing. The CDW linked up with another worker who knew the groups and networks within that area, and between them they advised the existing consortium to stop in their tracks and engage communities before progressing plans. The workers advised the consortium on a project plan which would enable it to check to what extent communities were on board and draw out communities' views on major decisions about what the development should contain, what it should look like and where it would best be placed on the site. The consortium is currently implementing the engagement plan.

Community development opens up whole new approaches to local issues through supporting communities to progress projects and activities that meet their identified needs and priorities. Sometimes these autonomous community activities then become the basis for decision making about releasing resources to further this development. In local authority systems, for example, which operate largely by written report and committee decision, community development workers write cabinet reports which are presented by their directors and agreed (or further information requested) by cabinet members. In this way collective approaches in communities spearheaded by residents' groups, parents' groups and so on become part of the corporate approach. This corporate commitment to development in the locality leads to the release or allocation of resources, and incorporation into agreements like the LAA.

> 'When it gets to a cabinet paper that means it's gone through lots of hoops, and cabinet will know that it has achieved certain standards and hit certain buttons. So they usually approve reports, or approve them subject to further information. So I know that that's a singularly effective route.'
>
> *Local authority practitioner*

> 'Through my involvement with the community we have been able to influence decisions within the authority positively for the benefit of the community.'
>
> *Local authority practitioner*

At this early stage in the life cycle of local area agreements, however, and in working with partners and services that are still inexperienced in engaging and empowering communities, community development workers' major contribution across the board in terms of improved decision making still seems to be about ensuring communities have a voice, and are listened to, rather than supporting campaigns about specific issues.

> 'It's not so much about working from the communities' concerns. It's taking a strategic need and seeing how community concerns can be reflected and can influence what the strategic thing becomes.'
>
> *CEN practitioner*

5 How can community development further amplify local governance and democracy?

Without exception, the practitioners who participated in our pilot study noted and welcomed the increasing policy focus on community empowerment and community engagement in local governance and democracy. They cited the 2006 Local Government White Paper (see footnote 4) as a major driver for their own and partner organisations to become more knowledgeable, skilled and effective at interacting with and understanding the communities they serve.

Nevertheless, some significant constraints on community development need to be recognised and addressed if the White Paper's vision of engaged communities is to be achieved, and if community development's potential to enhance local governance and democracy is to be realised. The actions needed to amplify community development's contribution to local governance and democracy are set out below.

Give community development the time it takes to build genuine and sustainable empowerment

The practice examples emphasised that intensive and long-term support is required genuinely to empower communities in a way that is sustainable. Community development research reports always make this point, because community development is rarely given enough time by funding streams, planning cycles or target setting.

In a local authority where community development is new, there is a new willingness to participate and a feeling that things can be changed for the better, but this has a long way to go before it translates to formal engagement in governance structures:

> 'Yes there is an informal group of residents who do something, who come out and take an interest, but they are not engaged in the governance. They're not now moving to participate on all the blocks as block leads on the LSP and they probably couldn't tell you what the local area agreement is or which block their work fits in.'
>
> *Local authority practitioner*

A community facility was established in one neighbourhood, offering service providers who wanted to deliver support locally the opportunity to use the facility for their outreach work. Some were enthusiastic about the facility at partnership tables, but gave up attending the facility after a couple of weeks if no one had attended. In contrast, a worker from a family support group came every week for the entire duration of the advertised session, bringing paperwork to do in case there were no enquiries or attendance. The worker attended for over a year in this way, and continues to do so. While there have been many weekly sessions with no one 'dropping in' at all, the group's head office has received a striking increase in phone enquiries from the neighbourhood, which have in turn led to meetings in the community hub and increased uptake in the service across the neighbourhood. The worker's continued presence and commitment to the neighbourhood has been noticed and responded to.

Quick fixes erode trust and disempower communities.

> 'There have been all these bodies who've said, "We've got funding and can make decisions and want community involvement." Then they will just go away. The exit strategy is "there's the key. See you later!" And local people are basically left high and dry. It's very much a case of, "We've seen it all before. Got the T-shirt. Got the socks. We'll believe it when we see it. You'll be gone in three years.".'
>
> *CEN practitioner*

Recommendations

- Central government, local government and other public agencies should commit themselves to long-term structures for funding community development, by reviewing and reorganising existing short-term funding streams.
- Central government should set, regional government should apply, and local government and partnerships should implement, realistic timescales for securing community engagement in regeneration and development programmes.
- Local government and other employers of community development workers should give practitioners time to build up trusting relationships and give engagement mechanisms and structures time to achieve maturity.

Promote better understanding of community development and engagement and resource internal development within local authorities

This pilot study echoed the findings of *The Community Development Challenge* report (see footnote 1) that community development is poorly understood at large, and even within authorities employing community development teams. Confusion exists about the difference between community development workers (who apply CD values and principles in their work, and apply six progressive components set out earlier in this report, in order to empower communities) and other officers, such as housing officers or community centre managers who deliver their service in communities. Community development teams are rarely managed by someone with community development knowledge and understanding, and community development can miss out on being something seen as very strategic and high level, or something fundamental about which all employees should have a basic awareness.

One practitioner felt disempowered by the lack of understanding of community development across her organisation. She felt there was no drive or enthusiasm for cultural change within her organisation, and that her own views on how things could be done differently were usually unwelcome and rejected. Whilst she was expected to act as a troubleshooter within communities, her professional opinion about what is achievable was not valued. This worker's experience will chime with other community development workers across the country. Nevertheless there were also examples in the study of community development workers' successful collective efforts to increase their impact on corporate approaches to working with communities.

Examples from the study suggest ways in which community development teams can restyle themselves effectively in order to promote a better understanding and wider application of community development across a local authority. Dedicating one community development team member to creating and delivering a rolling programme of learning opportunities for colleagues across the authority is one example. Learning opportunities range from induction materials for all employees to experiential training for officers and elected members.

Explicitly assigning one community development worker to support each service directorate with its community engagement needs seems a particularly powerful way of promoting better understanding and application of community engagement (if not development) across an authority. Placed alongside a responsibility for a particular geographical area, a neighbourhood renewal policy area and an underserved group, this assignment of a service area clearly puts an extra demand on workers' time and attention but, to some degree, the development of protocols for agreeing the parameters of boundary-spanning work protects workers from unrealistic expectations.

Where community development workers had access to directors and senior officers they were usually able to demonstrate how good community development achieved key targets in terms of corporate performance assessment, better decision-making processes and better decisions. Nevertheless workers can increase their effectiveness in securing buy-in from strategic colleagues by preparing themselves to meet strategic challenges.

> 'Everybody's job, whether it's about building roads or education, is about communities and people. And we've been in this area of work long enough to know how best to communicate with communities, and we needed to impart that knowledge internally. If we hadn't had the review and changed the team's direction we'd still be brought in to undertake the work because the [government] agenda says we have to, but we'd be far less sophisticated at working internally to help [services] come out to communities. We wouldn't have been asked to help develop the strategy for the council on how it moves forward locally. We would have missed all the opportunities to be included in shaping methods and approaches. We'd have been expected to jump without having developed those sorts of internal relationships and that understanding. But now we're able to say, "No, you've got that wrong", or "Hang on, there's somebody who says we need to do it a different way", or be more forceful in the use of the corporate approach to engagement that we have designed.'
>
> *Local authority practitioner*

Recommendations

- Community development umbrella organisations should provide better support to community development workers and strategic stakeholders in evidencing and articulating the strategic benefits of good community development practice.
- Community development workers should organise themselves collectively to maximise the impact of their knowledge and skills on the way their organisations and partners work with communities.
- Learning and development support should be provided for managers to enable them to recognise the knowledge and skills of their teams and maximise opportunities for these to be harnessed at strategic levels.

Recognise opportunity costs of focusing on engagement and resource appropriate development work in communities

> 'It's only by doing the whole lot [of the progressive components of community development] that you're doing community development, and what it made me concerned about was how much I am prompting engagement based on a legal requirement to have a community strategy and a local area agreement, and that's not just about community need.'
>
> *CEN practitioner*

Community development workers welcomed the policy context in which community engagement was given increasing importance, and were keen to find ways to demonstrate how community development supports strategic aims and corporate performance overall. Nevertheless the opportunity costs and diversionary effects of refocusing community development worker or team roles on community engagement are clear and considerable.

If workers prioritise engagement work (either within authorities or within communities), they withdraw some support that was previously offered to communities to work on their own issues and autonomous activities. Community development workers need to maintain robust links and trusting relationships with communities, or their advice on engagement will not be grounded in communities' experiences, needs and aspirations. They also need to ensure that another agency or authority is providing the level of intensive support that groups need in order to develop, network and engage.

This can be achieved through service level agreements (SLAs) with other tiers of government and with voluntary sector providers. By monitoring SLAs, community development workers can keep abreast of what support is available locally and what developments are underway. They can effectively signpost or broker relationships with other development workers when they can't respond to communities themselves. However, there is a double opportunity cost in relying on the voluntary and community sector (VCS), in particular, to provide support to communities on their autonomous activities. Not only is a large proportion of VCS time and activity necessarily spent securing funds and justifying funding spent on their development activities, but VCS organisations themselves are usually called into engagement processes because of their in-depth knowledge of community needs and aspirations. While the advocacy role of the VCS is both legitimate and important, it is not the same as providing community development support.

Recommendation

- All policies that invoke community empowerment or rely on community engagement should have a built-in margin of their budget allocated to community development and community capacity building.

Become increasingly sophisticated in the use of measures for evidencing influence

Community development improves decision-making processes and decisions made, but this can be hard to evidence, particularly if the change that community development makes is around boundary-spanning work across silos, or helping services to change their relationships with communities. What's more, communities can experience a gap between their ability to articulate their needs and ideas and the ability for that to influence a decision. By building on the introduction of indicators in community development and engagement, community development workers, statutory agencies, partners and communities themselves can begin to build a picture of where community development practice and community involvement result in change, and where the barriers to change exist.

Practitioners within the study welcomed those indicators embedded in official guidance on LAAs, which gauge whether people feel they can influence what goes on around them, and assess baseline levels of community activity and participation. One community development worker, a community activist and a strategic director all articulated the link between community development activity in a neighbourhood and higher ratings in these indicators. Community development workers are also developing evaluation tools such as the 'axis of influence' to use with communities to assess how ready for influencing they are, and how much influence their engagement is having on decisions. They are inserting additional indicators into LAAs, which they will use to hold partnerships to account if gaps emerge or persist between groups' engagement activities, skills and knowledge and their influence on decisions.

> 'It's almost a precautionary bargaining chip. If we work with our networks to help them understand how to evidence influence and how to achieve influence, and they feel that they are in a position to have influence, and if the circumstances are right to influence but it's still not clear what influence they are having, then I can go back to my partners and say, "We've got all these people coming together to try and promote change but there's a barrier to it which

is these officer or partner behaviours and attitudes." And my networks will be able to identify that.'

CEN practitioner

Recommendations

- Norms should be established for CD units, projects and practitioners to collect, as a routine part of their work, evidence of input and impact using recognised criteria, distinguishing CD input and the value added to outcomes by CD, and relating to the relevant indicators in performance management frameworks.
- Evaluation tools on influence should be used to support community groups, representatives and networks, to mark progress and hold partnerships to account for behaviours and attitudes which constrain change and development.

Appendix A

Methods

Pilot study aims

The study set out to demonstrate how community development amplifies community empowerment and participation in relation to local governance and democracy, and enhances the quality of that activity (in terms of inclusion, participation and sustainability.

Pilot study design

Because of the short timescale for carrying out the study – and the potentially infinite research topic – we designed the pilot in a particular way. Rather than attempting to analyse all aspects of a community development worker's practice, or to understand everything about the context in which CD workers are operating, we chose to focus our analysis on particular aspects of each worker's practice in relation to this topic. For example, the major focus of one practitioner's work might be providing support for community representatives to participate effectively (for example, in LSP meetings), in which case we would seek to analyse and understand that role in detail.

We sought the participation of five workers whose practice offered opportunities to study different aspects of community development practice in depth and distil learning. In such a small-scale project we did not intend that either the practitioners or their roles would be representative or comprehensive. Rather, we aimed to use a limited number of participants to generate insights on a cross-section of roles, approaches, impacts, success factors and challenges in relation to local governance and democracy.

Our preliminary list of practitioners to contact was based mainly upon advice from CDF colleagues. From around 15 initial approaches made, five practitioners confirmed that they were:

- practising community development
- undertaking activities in their work to empower communities and support community involvement in local governance and decision making
- available for, and willing to participate in, a research visit in July 2007.

Practitioners who ruled themselves out were undertaking policy work (not practice) on local governance and decision making, were undertaking tightly focused group development work in which local governance and decision making was a marginal, not a major focus, or were unavailable during the timeframe for the study.

Each of the five potential participants was then asked to answer a short checklist about the main focus of their local governance and democracy work ('aspects of practice question', see Appendix B) and the extent to which they were carrying out all six progressive components of community development ('components question', see Appendix B). The 'aspects of practice' question drew from previous work by CDF's Practice Links team on what community development workers can and should do to support leadership and representation and enhance local democracy. The 'components question' drew from the report *The Community Development Challenge* (see footnote 1).

By asking practitioners to reflect, in this way, on which aspects they focus on most or have the richest experience of in their work, we were able to ensure a spread of experiences and insights in relation to local governance and democracy.

- Providing support for community representatives to participate effectively (for example, in LSP meetings).
- Enabling community representatives to be accountable to their constituency.
- Encouraging a wider range of community members to become representatives.

- Stimulating and supporting community level debates and discussions.
- Promoting meaningful dialogue between communities and decision makers.
- Mediating tensions and conflicts between community leaders and councillors.
- Mediating divisions and dissent within and between communities.
- Supporting councillors to stimulate and access community debates, views and discussions.
- Supporting public authorities and partnerships to reach out into communities and stimulate involvement in deliberation and strategic planning.
- Setting up and servicing the structures and communication systems for ongoing community involvement and discussion.

The implications of their differing responses are discussed in Chapter 1 (pages 2–3).

Sources of information

Once participants had been identified in this way, we gathered and analysed documentary material provided by participants or sourced from (their own or their partner organisations') websites. This background information included individual, team and organisational action plans; monitoring plans and reports; project plans; committee reports; evaluation reports; organograms and team structures; journal articles; working group terms of reference; publicity leaflets and information packs; LAA briefings; community consultation results; a tenant and leadership participation compact; a community engagement and consultation strategy; and an axis of influence handbook.

The single largest and most important source of information was interviews with practitioners themselves. The interviews were semi-structured, reflective, face-to-face, and each lasted around two hours. The interviews addressed three broad themes:

- **Practitioners' role and activities**

  For example: What do community development workers do to enhance/amplify community empowerment in relation to local governance and democracy. What's their role in relation to the six key components of CD described in the CD challenge report? How do they practise? What is CD about the way they practise? What difference does doing this as a CD worker or in a CD way make to community empowerment?

  These questions aimed to focus on one or two aspects of practice in depth and detail but begin to place these aspects in the context of each worker's wider practice.

- **Impacts and influence of their practice**

  For example: What has changed as a result? Who has benefited from the change? How do they know their practice contributed to the change?

  The objective here was to prompt practitioners' reflections on the difference that their practice has made to the decision-making process and to the decisions that have been made.

- **Success factors and barriers**

  For example: What factors and conditions enable your community development work to contribute effectively to community empowerment? What has created difficulties and barriers to achieving 'good' community empowerment/engagement, and how have these problems been tackled? What have you learnt from your experience in this role that others might find useful?

  These questions aimed to place practitioners' experiences in their wider context and distil transferable knowledge and insights.

The same broad themes were then used in semi-structured phone interviews with other interviewees, lasting around half an hour each. By talking to other people we gathered perspectives from different people who have been involved in, supported by or challenged by empowered communities and empowerment processes, and were able to supplement and gain new perspectives on the material gathered from CD practitioners.

The exact wording of the questions differed to reflect interviewees' differing positions in the local governance and democracy landscape, and differing relationships to the CD practitioner (for example, as an activist being supported by them, a manager employing them, or a corporate client or partner using their expertise and knowledge). However the thrust of the questions remained the same.

- **Practitioners' role and activities**

  How do these aspects of practice relate to you? What did the practitioner do that helped/supported/affected or challenged you (or your work)? How would you describe the way he or she did it?

- **Impacts and influence of their practice**

  What has changed in terms of the decision-making process? How can you tell? Did the practice influence any decisions that have been made?

- **Success factors and barriers**

  What do you think has helped the practitioner to do what he or she did and make a difference? How and why did this enable the practitioner? What has created difficulties and barriers to achieving 'good' community empowerment/engagement and how have these been tackled? What have you learnt from [observing, supporting, partnering, etc. in this work?

Appendix B

Example checklist on 'aspects of practice'

Practitioner name:

1. We have put together a list of ten roles that practitioners have told us they undertake in relation to local governance and democracy. Which of the following are **major aspects of your practice** and might be a **fruitful focus for analysing your practice**?

   a. Providing support for community representatives to participate effectively (in LSP meetings, etc.).

   b. Enabling community representatives to be accountable to their constituency.

   c. Encouraging a wider range of community members to become representatives.

   d. Stimulating and supporting community level debates and discussions.

   e. Promoting meaningful dialogue between communities and decision makers.

   f. Mediating tensions and conflicts between community leaders and councillors.

   g. Mediating divisions and dissent within and between communities.

   h. Supporting councillors to stimulate and access community debates, views and discussions.

   i. Supporting public authorities and partnerships to reach out into communities and stimulate involvement in deliberation and strategic planning.

j. Setting up and servicing the structures and communication systems for ongoing community involvement and discussion.

List only the letters that are ***the most major*** *focus of your work, for example, a and b*

2. This research is a follow-on to the CD challenge report which defines community development as consisting of six progressive components. Can you **rank the components in order, starting with the component that you spend most time and attention on**? Omit any components that are carried out by colleagues or other team members rather than yourself.

A. Help people see that they have common concerns about local or other public issues and they could benefit from working on together under their own control.

B. Help people to work together on those issues, often by forming or developing an independent community group, supporting them to plan and take action and encourage evaluation and reflection as a way of improving effectiveness.

C. Support and develop independent groups across the community sector non-directively but within an ethical framework, and increase networking between groups.

D. Promote values of equity, inclusiveness, participation and co-operation throughout this work.

E. Empower people and their organisations to influence and transform public policies and services and all factors affecting the conditions of their lives.

F. Advise and inform public authorities on community perspectives and assist them to strengthen communities and work in genuine partnership with them.

Rank the roles in order starting with the most important in your practice. Only include roles you routinely undertake yourself, for example, E, C, B, A.

References

Cabinet Office (2001) *A New Commitment to Neighbourhood Renewal: National Strategy Action Plan*: London, Cabinet Office.

CDF, CDX, FCDL and CD2 Working Group (2006) *The Community Development Challenge*: London, Department of Communities and Local Government.

Communities and Local Government (2006) *Strong and Prosperous Communities: The Local Government White Paper*: London, Communities and Local Government

Federation for Community Development Learning and PAULO (2003) *National Occupational Standards for Community Development Work*: Sheffield, Federation for Community Development Learning/PAULO